Everything You Want

the *secrets* behind
THE LAW OF ATTRACTION

MUNEEZA KHIMJI

© Copyright 2007 Muneeza Khimji.

Edited by Joti Bryant
Cover by Yvonne Koo

All rights reserved. No part of this publication may be reproduced, stored in a retrieval system, or transmitted, in any form or by any means, electronic, mechanical, photocopying, recording, or otherwise, without the written prior permission of the author.

Note for Librarians: A cataloguing record for this book is available from Library and Archives Canada at www.collectionscanada.ca/amicus/index-e.html

ISBN 1-4251-1802-x

Printed in Victoria, BC, Canada. Printed on paper with minimum 30% recycled fibre. Trafford's print shop runs on "green energy" from solar, wind and other environmentally-friendly power sources.

Offices in Canada, USA, Ireland and UK

Book sales for North America and international:
Trafford Publishing, 6E–2333 Government St.,
Victoria, BC V8T 4P4 CANADA
phone 250 383 6864 (toll-free 1 888 232 4444)
fax 250 383 6804; email to orders@trafford.com

Book sales in Europe:
Trafford Publishing (UK) Limited, 9 Park End Street, 2nd Floor
Oxford, UK OX1 1HH UNITED KINGDOM
phone 44 (0)1865 722 113 (local rate 0845 230 9601)
facsimile 44 (0)1865 722 868; info.uk@trafford.com

Order online at:
trafford.com/07-0214

10 9 8 7 6 5 4 3 2

CONTENTS

Acknowledgments
xi

Foreword
xiii

Introduction
1

Chapter 1
The Mind
7

Chapter Summary
13

Chapter 2
Beliefs
15

Chapter Summary
23

Chapter 3
Concept of The Self and the Black Box
25

Chapter Summary

32

Chapter 4
Feelings & Intentions

33

Chapter Summary

41

Chapter 5
Visualization

43

Chapter Summary

53

Chapter 6
Letting Go

55

Chapter Summary

61

Chapter 7
Negative Self Talk

63

Chapter Summary

69

Conclusion
71

Chapter Summary
74

Methods of Learning
75

Extended Exercises/Methods
79

Glossary
83

This book is dedicated to those who have
the passion and the desire to unlearn.

"Keep your thoughts positive because your thoughts become your words

Keep your words positive because your words become your behavior

Keep your behavior positive because your behavior becomes your habits

Keep your habits positive because your habits become your values

Keep your values positive because your values become your destiny."

—Mohandas Mahatma Gandhi

Acknowledgments

I would like to give special thanks to the forces that inspired me to write this book.

There are a number of people who have supported me and to whom I would like to give credit. First and foremost my husband, Fayaz Ladha for his kindness, patience and passion for the undertaking of this book and our lives as a whole. Your commitment to us is inspiring.

To my father and my siblings who, without a doubt, are the best cheering squad for any and all of my projects, thank you for your unconditional love. All my love and gratitude to my beautiful niece Sophia, for always keeping my spirits high.

To my mother, who is here to share this in spirit. You are my *raison d'être*. I miss you always.

I would like to give special recognition to Joti Bryant, my editor who helped me find the words when I could no longer find them; to Yvonne Koo, my graphic designer who has created a delightful cover and put a picture to my thought. Thank you both, for your dedication to this project and your hard work.

To my publisher at Trafford publishing, you have made this process easy and enjoyable.

Last but not least I would like to thank my teacher, for striving to bring me to greater heights of understanding; Dr. James Polisak. Your insight, persistence and patience is much appreciated.

Foreword

I began writing this book over two years ago, inspired to share with others what I have learnt, and further inspired to teach those in search of a dream life. I started it several times and wrote many drafts, discarding one after the other. I still had much of my own process to complete. I continued on my journey, but always came back to writing this, and yet I was never quite ready. I was waiting for my moment of clarity. Today it came. And so I began.

This book began as a method of self-teaching. As I was learning many new things about myself and my skills and talents I began to document my findings, awakenings, realizations, epiphanies, and of course a ton of negative emotions that I will not get into!

Eventually I decided that my journey of learning was one that I wanted to share with the world. Most especially I wanted to share the amazing concepts I have incorporated into my life, for these have changed who I am, and continue to change me on a regular basis.

As a result of learning how the Law of Attraction works and the ups and downs of the change process, I acquired a number of tools - to help me along and to facilitate the process. It is these tools, the knack of staying positive, as well as understanding what holds us back and why, that I wanted to share with the world, not just the joy of using this law to create the life we want.

I began my journey 10 years ago, whilst in university. (I will not tell you which degree or year, as I am sure you are smart enough to calculate my age!) Suffice to say, it was a journey of tremendous ups and downs. I began to learn the art of visualizing: tapping into my abilities to project and attract (sending out thoughts in the form of energy, attracting back what I am thinking of) the experiences, friends, and relationships I desire in my life.

It was a challenge to learn to look at myself in a whole new light and from a totally new perspective. For years I could not see that the wars I was fighting within myself were also the wars that were always played out around me and mirrored in my relationships, my friends, my home, my work. Slowly, as I continued on, (and on many a day felt lost), did I come to understand the power of my mind and my innate abilities. I began to understand that everything that I experienced, both good and bad, I attracted. I began to accept the idea that I can have anything I want, and the only person that dictates who I am, is me.

To sum up that realization in such few words does not do

justice to the joys and the pain of such a journey. Nonetheless, I am here today wiser and smarter, and without a doubt, happier and more fulfilled.

In this voyage of learning about me, I had to shed all that I thought I knew, and all that I liked, about myself. Getting rid of the positive things was harder than the negative because, (and only hindsight taught me this,) what was seemingly positive at that time were only negative thoughts and feelings, enveloped in a cloud of positivity. This was a huge realization into how deep negativity runs within the human psyche.

And so with my teacher by my side, and my husband cheering me on, I embarked on my expedition and began to open my black box. In doing so I let go of many beliefs that I thought were mine, but in fact were just blindly accepted by me. I had to get to know the real me, defense mechanisms and all. There have been many ups and downs, but I have not spoken to many about them, nor do I feel the need to.

I do however want to acknowledge the trials, as they are a part of my process, and a stepping-stone to my success.

Now as daunting as this process sounds, it was actually worse than I can find the words to describe! However, I look at where I am today and am thankful for having worked through the cobwebs in my mind. The relevance? Simply this, when I set out to visualize a goal there were times it did not manifest. I now understand that my subconscious can obstruct my visualizations and did so. Although what I wanted was seemingly good, for whatever reason, at times my subconscious stopped it, as (I understand now) it thought it was protecting me.

Let me give you a small example. I had misconceptions about money - like ninety nine percent of the population on the planet. I believed many limiting things about money, and though I would visualize making more, more would not materialize - because I believed that there had to be something unique happening, to be in the position of making that money. Thus, no matter what I visualized, my subconscious believed I was not that unique, so therefore did not deserve the money. As a result I was not able to attract more money.

Upon learning that my black box was limiting me, in more ways than I can ever explain, with my teacher, I began to tear it apart and face everything that was inside it. I began to speak my truth, and even though most was heard only by me, I released it, and freed myself.

I know you are asking now, "What is the black box and why is it so important?" The black box is a part of the subconscious mind, and in it is every negative association that you have created, in response to the entire world around you. It is your understanding of and your relationship with money, people, fear, success, failure and growth, and everything else that you can think of. It is what makes you frustrated and sad; it is what determines how successful you will be at creating change, as well as accepting it.

And so going into the black box is imperative, for it is a very important part of your subconscious, and it is on this level where you attract the life you want. In your black box are your defense mechanisms, every heartbreak, all grief and every fear, (however imperceptibly small), brought out under a magnifying glass.

The black box is dealing with and confronting everything that hurt you in your life, along with everything that you sabotaged, resisted, or did not deal with. Your subconscious mind was always protecting you, so you never felt the need to face this part of your mind. Releasing and resolving what is in it, involves healing at the root level.

In the time between beginning writing this book, and its completion, many more wonderful resources have come to light, such as "The Secret" and "What The Bleep Do We Know?" These have inspired me even more to share my knowledge. Both these resources are available at your local bookstore or online at www.amazon.com and other sites. (Just type "The Secret" or "What the Bleep" into your search engine, Google, Yahoo, AOL, etc., for a full listing.)

My goal is to make this book a simple tool to enable you to understand your personal mechanisms and yourself. The exercises are designed to clear out the old you, whilst you create the new you! Have fun, for this is where you get to choose who you want to be!

We all have a black box. I encourage you to open it, and face what is in it, using the tools to better yourself, using the same tools to visualize what it is you want for your dream life. I encourage you to exorcise the cobwebs of your mind.

I also encourage you to seek the support of a friend, a loved one, mentor, or a coach, anyone who can be your cheerleading squad and a shoulder throughout your journey. There is no reason for you to have to resolve your past on your own. The support will help you clear out your black box more efficiently and more quickly.

Through this you will learn to speak your truth and begin

sculpting your life. All of the areas this book covers help you to access your black box, as well as to create a positive, focused, intentioned life for yourself.

The exercises at the back are designed to keep you on course and encouraged. Use them often, as they will support you through this journey of enlightenment and change.

Introduction

The literature that is available today on the mind, and the psychology of it, is available in abundance, and the basic foundations of psychology are easily grasped by most. The functioning of the mind however and the abilities that each of us possess, are not as well known.

Each and every one of us is born with the skills and the abilities that this book will help to enhance. These are skills that are innate and only need to be cultivated in order to create the life that you want.

What is the 'Power of Now? It is the power that each person possesses, regardless of status, creed, financial standing, religion and education. It is the gift of the mind and the universe, the power to use the mind to achieve anything we can imagine. Using our minds in this way allows us to climb a mountain, or clean a room, by simply seeing it mentally, first.

The power comes into effect when you become skilled at using these tools; you are then in unity with the universe, as you should be. This is the power of now, and the level at which I hope you continue to grow.

The skills that I refer to are those that most of us don't even know we have. The ability to visualize, the ability to manifest, and the power of words. Your current life experience is the product of your every thought and feeling to-date.

You have consistently, whether you know it or not, employed the Law of Attraction, and as a result all your successes and all of your failures, are the result of your individual thoughts and feelings.

In employing this Law, you have also attracted things you do not want. The aim here is for you to understand this Law and learn its uses, so you will continue to employ this Law, but more consciously, so that now you attract what you want.

There are two ways to accomplish a task: mentally or physically. When you complete a task physically, for example apply for a job, you can only do so one way. After updating your resume, you apply for postings you like and then decide whether to mail, deliver by hand, or e-mail. You can only make an application for a job with one of the above methods.

By visualizing your end goal, the job, you are in fact commanding the Universe; it will then guide you to complete the best way to apply for the job that is perfect for you, and the specific job, instead of randomly applying for dozens, in the hopes of scoring "the right one". Then you may be "lucky" and bump into the "right person" when dropping off your resume, or when e-mailing it the person you are writing to will have a few extra minutes to respond to your application right away. The possibilities of how incidents will line up to assist you are endless.

Using this method does not imply you will not have to do anything physically, but simply that you will be in the right place at the right time and your actions will facilitate the desired result.

When you see in your mind what you want, you are in fact leaving the process open to any and all possibilities, which is more likely to get you to your goal successfully, and faster than only doing it the normal physical way.

The best way I have heard it described it this: "The "hows" are the domain of the universe. It always knows the shortest, quickest, fastest, most harmonious way between you and your dream." 'The Secret', Mike Dooley,

The purpose of this book is to show you how you can create the life you want — by using this Law and employing it with intention. It is a step-by-step guide for removing the negative and introducing the positive in a way that every day, every moment, not only do you feel excited, inspired and awake; you are eager to face new challenges.

If you stop and look at your life, like most people on the planet you probably have plenty to be grateful for, a lot to be thankful for, and yet there is a large part of the puzzle missing.

We search for this piece of the puzzle through religion, philosophy, spiritual practices, self-improvement courses, and dieting, to name a few. The fact is that in all that we search for we have yet to find the solace that we so desire. We have yet to find the missing piece.

You are born in a great universe, that is filled with abundance, and you are here to enjoy every moment of it. If you are not happy and enjoying it, then you are not living the life that you really want. By directing your thoughts, you can be as happy as you want, (or as unhappy as you want); only you can be the commander of change.

This is a universe that responds to feelings. Thoughts generate feelings and all humans possess an abundance of feelings. We also have the gift of imagination. When we imagine something we first feel the energy of it, and then manifest it.

The process is so simple and yet so complex; its complexity arises from the simple fact that our minds can no longer see the simplicity behind this idea, for we have become overwhelmed by society's rules on how to live. "Simple" does not fit into the belief that "life is a struggle" and having things that are worthwhile should involve experiencing discomfort or pain. These erroneous beliefs are widely accepted by many, thus simple concepts such as the one outlined above are quickly rejected.

Whether we are religious or not, most of us have been taught that we humans were created in the image of God. But what we weren't taught is that we were also given the ability to attract and manifest anything we want. So we have managed to create mostly what we don't want! Regardless of your own religion or beliefs, you will quickly see the irony behind this.

Your first task, and perhaps the most difficult, is while reading this, to let go of how you think the world should be and how you think your life should be, and instead focus on what you want it to be. Notice how different these two pictures are. This is the discrepancy your whole life is based upon.

The things that happen to you are not always what you want, nor all of what you don't want, but perhaps something in the middle of the two. This is the result of the discrepancy between how you think your life should be and how you want it to be. When you become clearer on what you want, the life you *want to have* will show up, and the life you thought you *should have* will disappear. I encourage you to take that step now, and open your mind to the possibilities - that are endless, and you will see your life take on a whole new meaning.

Remember, when you make a change in one aspect of your life, this dominos into all other areas of your life. When you make a positive change in one area of your life, such as develop better communication with your workmates this has a ripple affect in other parts of your life. You will find that you are communicating better with your spouse and your friends; your ability to understand others also increases. This in turn makes you visibly more empathetic towards others, and could result in a job promotion, better relationships, and many more positive things.

In conjunction with this material, I strongly recommend watching the documentary "The Secret" if you have not done so already. It is a fabulous visual of many of the same concepts explained here. (For information on where to find this resource, please refer to the Foreword.)

I encourage you to read this book right through to the end. Then, and only then, will you have given this information a fair chance, and yourself a fair chance. As simple as most of this is, it will take time and practice to learn to use it effectively. But most certainly you will learn, and be amazed by the results.

As you read this book, and enjoy other resources that will come your way to facilitate change in your life, you will see changes within you and around you. As part of the change process I encourage you to make a distinction between the "old you" and the "new you". This is a distinction that will come in handy as you do the following exercises, and the value will become clearer as you read on.

At the end of this book there is a section called 'Methods of Learning' which you can use to support you in this process and help you to make permanent changes. The exercises are designed to remove old ways of thinking and create new ones. Use them as often as you can and apply them to all aspects of your life.

Remember, life does not happen to you. You happen to life. You have the power, by utilizing the methods covered in this book, to create the life you want. Everything that you are is a result of how you subconsciously chose to use and work with this power up until now.

This is the time to make different, better, more conscious choices!

1

The Mind

The human mind is a complex and yet fascinating piece of machinery that, like a computer, can run several programs at once. It is by far the best computer out there today.

There are many different theories on the mind, especially its make-up and function. Suffice to say; most theorists are still discovering its mysteries.

Having a Freudian background, this explains my own version of the way the mind works. Nonetheless, the universal agreement is that in order to understand the mind we must first look at human behavior. Now, I am not going to give more than the basic explanation here for this theory, as it can get complicated, and more than the basics is not relevant.

According to Freudian theory, and I agree with this, (as do many theorists), the mind is made up of three parts: the conscious, the pre-conscious and the subconscious. Our concern here lies with only two parts: the conscious and the subconscious. Since learning the theory, in my continued work as a therapist and ongoing learning as a professional, I have determined in part, my own understanding of the mind. Some may say this is a collection of theories, and it may be. However, this is the theory by which I learn, and which I use in my practice. The key areas are the two parts of the mind mentioned earlier.

The conscious mind is exactly that - your conscious, (aware), thoughts, feelings, and perceptions, on a day-to-day basis. The subconscious mind is the part of your mind that contains, I believe, the wisdom of the world and all the knowledge there is to gain. It is where your spirit is housed; it is your higher self, or whatever other terminology you use to describe the more spiritual and greater part within you. In this part of the mind is also a phenomenon known as your gut instinct. This part of the brain also contains all the positive emotions and feelings that guide you and drive you in life.

Now within this part of the mind is also what I refer to as the "black box". (As mentioned in the Foreword.) This is every negative perception you have of the world: all the heartache, all the grief, pain, suffering, bad thoughts, including all of the negative experiences you have had in your life. This box also contains your negative and limiting beliefs.

I do not believe that the whole of the subconscious mind is negative, or contains all of your negative experiences, for if this were true change would not be possible. I do believe that this is a small portion, that along with the conscious mind, guides your behavior.

Now I am sure you are wondering about the importance

and significance of this. Bear with me, we will get there in due course!

The reason most people create change in their lives and find it temporary at best, is simply because when they effect change they do so only on a conscious level.

In order to be completely successful it is necessary to first work at the root, or subconscious level. Therefore the black box must be opened and the contents worked with and resolved, in order to have change be completely effective, on every level. The basic reason is this: all of your behavior stems from beliefs and programming received through life – the black box is the repository of all the limiting and/or negative input and ideas.

If you believe you cannot achieve something perhaps it is because at some point in your life you tried but did not succeed. This belief will continue to work against you, no matter how many times you try. However, if you remove this limiting belief, there is a strong chance that you can now achieve this thing, since that which was stopping you is no longer there. You now believe you can, and so will, attract that very thing to you. I will go into more detail later on in the book about beliefs and their limitations.

The mind does not know the difference between what is real and what is visualized, nor does it know the difference between something that is large versus something that is small. These are perceptions that we have driven into our psyche. Also the idea of something being hard to accomplish, versus something that is easy. Again this is a false root belief. If we have tried and not succeeded it is less destructive to the self/ego to see that task as hard to accomplish.

These perceptions then become the models and the concepts by which we understand the world around us. We use these models to filter information from our environment and fit into our concept of the world. The fact is that our models can be wrong, and so when we attempt to change we are not successful because the model does not work.

Let's go back to the previous statement. The mind does not know the difference between an event that is real versus one that is imagined. Athletes preparing to run a race who do so only in their mind, have been found to fire the same muscles in the very same sequence as if they were actually physically running the race.

Thus, if the mind does not know the difference between whether you are running the race in reality or not, then this is where your creative mechanism comes in. If there is no difference, then there is no harm in actually determining something that you do want, and visualizing it, therefore being consciously creative. This is the way in which your mind was created to work: to determine what you want and magnetize it, rather than abide by models that may not be right for you.

The human mind works in pictures. In other words when you think of something, perhaps the color pink, then your mind is in fact seeing the color pink, or whatever the relationship of pink is in your mind. For example, the color pink in your mind may represent a particular flower from your childhood, or a certain type of food that you like or dislike. So, when you think of the color pink, more often than not you are seeing the picture associated with it, rather than the color itself.

Here is another important fact. The mind also does not know the difference between the words "do" and "do not". In other words, when you tell yourself that you are not going to do something, you are still giving your mind an instruction, a picture; it does not understand the word no. The mind is goal-oriented and thus can only focus on each goal or picture being presented to it. By saying either yes or no to what you want, you are creating a picture, and sending an order to your mind. This is another reason many people find that they are saying no to something, and surprisingly it still manifests!

Let's take an example to clarify that. The child who dislikes the man that his father has become, who firmly decides at a young age that he will not become anything like his father, without realizing it, is giving instructions to his mind to become like his father. His mind takes this goal, as it cannot differentiate between "shall" and "shall not". Twenty years later he realizes he has become that which he thought he strived so hard not to be: his father.

So when you say you do or do not want to do something, either way you are creating a picture in your mind, you are visualizing that very thing. By saying "no" you are still reinforcing that as a goal. In order for the young man not to become like his father, he needs to re-visualize himself, with qualities unlike his father, and not simply say "no". The mind does not hear "no".

Every human is born this way, with all the skills and tools I have mentioned thus far, and those I have yet to mention. When you see something in your mind, you are engaging the Law of Attraction. What you think about most, you will attract, whether it is what you want or what you do not want.

What you focus on becomes yours— regardless of whether it is good or bad.

Your mind was not created to judge, but simply as a goal-striving mechanism. It was designed to follow your commands for what you want. You see in pictures what you want, and along with the feelings associated, you attract what you decide you want.

In exactly the same way, when you do not want something, with the same mechanism, you see it, and although you may say vehemently that it is something you do not want, you still attract it, for you are placing the power of your emotions behind it.

Through reading this book and doing the exercises to come, you will re-learn how to see only what you want, and not have to make the distinction between that which you want and that which you do not want.

Now that you have an understanding of how your mind works and the importance of the positive versus the negative, you can begin your journey; a spiritual journey, for you are now *consciously* creating the life that you want.

CHAPTER SUMMARY

- Ø You attract on the conscious and the subconscious levels.
- Ø Understanding the black box allows you to attract on every level what you want.
- Ø The mind does not know the difference between a real or an imagined event.
- Ø Your mind works in pictures. Create a picture of what you want in order to attract exactly what you desire.
- Ø When you want to change a picture in your mind, re-visualize and keep the new picture.
- Ø What you think about most you attract, whether it is positive or negative.
- Ø Your mind is a goal-striving mechanism, designed to fulfill your goals.

2

Beliefs

Our beliefs are our guiding mechanisms that allow us to determine whether or not we can accomplish a task, and whether or not we will be successful at this task. These mechanisms are usually created from the sum of all life experiences, as well as the more significant people in our lives: parents, teachers, religious leaders and partners.

I am sure you are now wondering how or why this is important. Not to worry, the answer will come soon!

Our beliefs also help define us, as we all define ourselves in part, by whether we can or cannot accomplish something. How does this engage the Law of Attraction you ask?

When you believe that you can or cannot do something, you are in fact projecting that belief. All things around us feel our energy. The energy that you emit is composed of your thoughts and feelings. All your thoughts and feelings stem from your beliefs about whether or not you can accomplish a particular task, or have a specific thing. So if you believe that you cannot complete said task, or acquire a desired object, you hold that thought, and feel it, and in turn it is projected. If you project the impossibility of successfully accomplishing a task, all that will happen is that you create exactly that, and you fail. What you think about is what you attract.

Let's take an example of this. If you believe that (and I know this is based on education and experience) you can only earn $500 a month, no matter what you visualize you cannot make more, because your beliefs hold you back. Let's take this one step further and assume the reason you do not earn more is because you believe you are not worthy of it. No matter what you visualize, no matter how much money you visualize, it will not materialize, for you do not believe you deserve it. Here is where your beliefs (conscious or subconscious) sabotage the process.

In order to truly change, and be attracting what you want, your beliefs - on both a conscious and subconscious level - have got to be in alignment with one another, otherwise the subconscious will more often than not win, as it is more powerful, and has a filtering system, which is designed to protect you. It automatically blocks change, or things coming to you, if they are not in alignment with your core beliefs.

In other words, you truly must *believe* you are worthy of making more money, and when you do so at a root level, as you visualize, whatever you see will manifest. Now the subconscious sees the value of what you are asking for, and does not block the manifesting process, in order to protect you from being disappointed and losing more faith in yourself, which occurs when you see yourself as not being worthy.

The above example is with the exception of beginners luck! Some people may find that despite their root level (subconscious mind) not being in alignment with their conscious mind, they may still be able to, on the one-off chance, attract more money, or whatever it is they are visualizing.

Invariably, this thinking will revert itself, and once again you will find that the root personality and desires are attracting most of what is appearing in your life. In other words, your subconscious beliefs, limiting ones included, will kick in again, and like an elastic band, pull you back from achieving having more money. The subconscious will always pull you back, no matter what. Thus, success can come once, but without change at the root level, you are not likely to see more money again until you change the limiting belief.

Now, when you decide to change your life and visualize different things for yourself, you are still doing it within the parameters of your belief system. If you want to attract more wealth, and visualize receiving more money, you need to do so knowing what your boundaries are.

Thus if you have beliefs that are negative and limiting, that is exactly what you will attract back into your life. Therefore, what you believe, you visualize; you then project and attract the same back to you, based on your specific beliefs.

The thing that most people do not know, or pay attention to, is that your beliefs can be changed, and most of the ones you have now have been given to you by the society and culture in which you live. Most of these you have not chosen, so now is the time to take the steps and decide which beliefs you want to keep and which you do not.

To do this you must also challenge the models of the world which you live by and therefore use as a guide for your life. This goes back to the concept we mentioned earlier of change at the root level. You can choose your own belief system, and not blindly follow what you think you should, such as religion. In following an idea that you do believe in you are attracting, at the root level, the things you truly want and desire.

Models of behavior are created by several systems working together. Basic models of relationships are formed from the bonds forged with our parents or guardians when we were children. In other words we learn how relationships between a man and a woman work from watching the way our parents interact, as well as from the way our father and mother interacted with us. Our models are also influenced by TV and other outside factors as well as what we believe. Thus our beliefs and our models work hand-in-hand in creating the environment in which we live.

These models act as filters and help us assimilate information from our environment. Now, if the model on which we are basing our theories is incorrect then most certainly our beliefs are incorrect and we are, absolutely, attracting into our lives, based on a faulty model.

The key is to decide who you want to be and then create the new you. The old you, with those beliefs, has attracted the people you currently have in your life, the relationships, the job. You have attracted all these things in part through your beliefs. The key is to change what you believe, by looking at your models and your definitions of the world, and how you operate within it. Just as our behavior tells us how the mind is functioning, models tell us which belief systems and mechanisms are currently at work.

Now because you are changing the way you think, and employing this Law, does not mean you will suddenly lose all your friends and have to change jobs, or that dramatic changes will occur so that you no longer recognize your life! All this means is that you will weed out those who are negative and not in alignment with your new way of thinking. In turn you will attract more friends who think like you.

I have heard many a time, women complain about the men they meet, and some especially, complain about the fact that they are constantly attracting the same "type" of person. Again, this goes back to the models of what a man should be, the belief that they deserve only a certain type or kind of man. Based on that, and their past men, they continue to visualize this 'type' and wonder why the same kind of man keeps showing up.

If they changed their idea of the "type" of man they want, and focused on the qualities they desire, they would find the person they truly want coming into their life. If they also understood why they seem to be, by default, attracted to a man that they do not want, perhaps they would see that this is a model from childhood that needs updating or changing.

Now comes the fun part. Changing this way of functioning! In order to determine what beliefs you want to keep and what you want to erase, I recommend you first make a list of all these beliefs. As seemingly new ones show up, add them to the list. Alternatively, you can simply look at your models of the world; these too will help you determine your beliefs. Let's take an example.

If you had a childhood where you were constantly let down and led to believe that people as a general rule are not trustworthy, you would find yourself becoming suspicious of everyone you meet. And if you look at your life I am sure you would find an inordinately high number of non-trustworthy people around you on a regular basis. Again your model of people came from your childhood, including your belief that people cannot be trusted. You then perceive many of the people in your life as fitting into this same mold.

By using the same process, in reverse, you examine the model which brought you to this point: how you engage with others, as well as your belief system, and then make the changes you want.

Take a good look at the list you have made, once you have decided which ones you no longer want, you need to see yourself with new ones. Once you visualize and begin this process you attract different and new people and things into your life, and slowly you become a new you. It is impossible to take everything and change in one day, however, I encourage you to isolate the more significant ones, and begin with those. Visualize them every day, and let them go, until you see the changes manifested. Once a change has become a part of you, you can move on to the next item.

Another law then comes into effect here, which is fabulous for the change process, called the Domino Effect. The Domino Effect is simply this, when you make changes in one area of your life, it affects all other areas of your life and begins change in those areas, whether you are aware of it. As the effects domino into other areas of your life, the overall change needed is decreased. So the characteristics, and the beliefs you need to change over time become less and less!

In other words, as you change your idea of your self worth, and if it is say focused on a building confidence, over a short period of time you will find that not only are you feeling more confident, but the people you interact with are more confident; you also attract new people who are more confident.

Other than visualizing, another fascinating method of change is change whilst in the moment. When you respond to your environment it is usually based again, on your beliefs.

It is common, whether you know it or not, when someone is passionately relaying a story to you regarding someone else, that you feel they are in fact talking about you. For example: You come home from work and your spouse begins to relay a story to you about a co-worker. Not realizing this is connected to a belief you hold, you take it personally, and it becomes an argument, leaving you both angry and frustrated. The first question you need to ask yourself is "How did I attract this?"

The answer is this: you took your spouse's story personally and believed there was something to complain about, saw it that way and in turn reacted to it. The change that can be executed in the moment that is so profound is this, the next time *stop for a moment,* and do not react at all!

What you are then doing is not allowing that old belief to come forth and attract more fights, (what you don't want), but to allow you time to mull over your reaction. As a result you are actively changing the belief, by not engaging with it.

To effect change like this, take any or all aspects of your life, and simply change the way you respond. The more calm and non-reactive you are, the less you are engaging any old beliefs, and so you begin to interact in a new and positive way. *The key is to remain calm.*

Using the above method has another advantage. You are using emotions to help the change process; this is a powerful tool that will continue to domino as you use all the other tools mentioned in this book.

As a part of change I encourage you to be gentle with yourself. Like all processes you will oscillate, but in time you will end up more on the side that you want to be on. Again, be kind to yourself, as you will face some resistance within to this process. Over time it will become more manageable. For more tips on how to handle and overcome the resistance read on!

CHAPTER SUMMARY

- Ø Whatever you believe, you are right, and this you will manifest and fulfill.
- Ø What you truly believe you project and therefore attract back to you.
- Ø Your subconscious and conscious minds need to be in alignment to attract what you want on a continuous basis.
- Ø What you visualize and attract is based on your beliefs.
- Ø The Domino Effect will allow you to change one area of your life, in turn effecting change in all other areas of your life.

3
Concept of The Self and the Black Box

The next step, as a part of this process, is to understand the concept of the self. It is important to recognize that the person you see yourself to be is a combination of characteristics others have pointed out about you, as well as the reactions you receive when you interact with the world around you.

Similarly, the concept of the self is also determined by the inside world and the outside world of each individual. Simply put, because you have made changes to the outside world, or your external self, does not mean that you have made any changes to the inside world. Remember our goal here is to effect change in both simultaneously.

Patients who undergo plastic surgery for a flaw they feel is clearly visible and has caused them emotional pain, who, after surgery do not change their mental image to fit their new external image, still feel as though that flaw exists and continue to behave in a way that indicates that.

Let's take an example to illustrate this point better. Take a man who has a scar on his cheek and is very self-conscious about it. This is a scar that has been there all his life. As a child he was ridiculed for it and mocked. As an adult he feels as though he has been rejected from relationships as a result of his scar. He has low self-esteem and sees himself as a failure in most areas of his life and most certainly in relationships. He goes for plastic surgery, and the scar is no longer there. He now goes out into the world with his new face, but still finds that many of the same things are happening to him. He is still being rejected by women and in turn is still feeling miserable about himself and his life.

What happened here is that this man did not align his new face with a new mental picture of himself. He continued to behave as though he still had a scar on his face and so believed that people still mocked him and stared at him as though he still had the scar. He still projected an image of himself as it was before surgery, and in turn attracted back others reacting to that very same image, as they had always done.

Had he re-aligned his mental picture of himself after surgery, he would have felt confident that he had changed and was different; in turn he would have projected this, and attracted people who accept him as he is now, and do not see the scar; just as he no longer sees it.

Once again the focus here is on aligning your inner world and your outer world, so that your subconscious is not overriding your conscious desires and visualizations.

If you recall, we mentioned the black box earlier and the significance of it. We focused on how this box is created and what is in it, and touched on some of the ramifications it has in your life. There is a black box in each of us. For some it is filled with hardships and pain; for others it is not as bad. That is not to say this is not painful to each and every one of us, it certainly is, however the depth of each person's pain varies, based on their life experiences.

In order to move forward in the change process, regardless of whether you are changing one part of you or all of you, the black box must be unearthed and dealt with. This is, again, the part of you that has all your defense mechanisms.

Your defense mechanisms are born from your interaction with the environment, or certain people in it, and the negative experiences you have had. Within the black box is contained your definition and concept of yourself, and your limiting behaviors.

The black box affects the way in which you engage with the world. Here originates the experience of self-sabotaging. Thus it is important to open this box and free all that is in there that is stopping you from achieving success.

Most of us are totally unaware of this space inside us, and much less that we operate with the entire world based on the material (beliefs, etc.) in this space. As an example take a child born into a wealthy family; she is pampered and spoilt and truly provided with everything as in most cases and as a result of being spoilt she has received no discipline and so she learns to provide herself with discipline. Later on in life, her parents now attempt to discipline her and advise her on how to complete a task. She takes offense to this, not because she cannot take the advice but more because she has already learnt to accomplish tasks on her own and feels her methods are now being criticized. As a result her parents no longer say anything, for when they do she flies off the handle.

Now, she meets someone and wants to settle down and get married. When her husband, (who is modeled on her relationship with her father, thus the reason she chose him) now attempts to advise her on how to complete a task, she reacts in the same way. She learnt to teach herself how to do things, and being told otherwise is an insult to her progress. This pattern is sitting in her black box and so as she engages with the world she finds that she is following the same pattern as with her parents.

I am aware that the above is a very in-depth example on behavior and I do not by any means expect you to be able to dissect your behaviors and black box in the same way. However, it is imperative that in unearthing this space in your mind you do so with some support, as mentioned earlier. It is extremely valuable to have this support, as well as a professional who is able to help you dissect your patterns and shed light on them, without you having to fight yourself in order to understand them.

If you recall, in Chapter two, we focused on beliefs and the models by which we understand the world. Again, the negative ones are housed in the black box and do need to be exorcised.

The emotions and experiences that we are hiding in the black box are the wars that we are fighting internally, which get projected and thus need to be resolved. Many people suffer from a lack of confidence and if you do not have confidence in yourself, no matter how much you battle it, you will exude this lack of confidence. In turn you will find that others do not have confidence in you, bosses, co-workers, friends, partners. You see them reflecting your war; because you projected it.

With that same logic comes another, higher understanding of the self. Every time something or someone upsets you or hurts you, it is always, and without exception, based on how you see the world. You have perceived a particular trigger to be emotional and upsetting.

Thankfully we do not all have the same triggers, or else this world would be filled with only one type of person. Nonetheless, your trigger is based on the emotions in the black box and you get upset because you feel insulted or let down. This is a trigger that you have perceived to be upsetting, regardless of what the cause is. This again is you functioning and attracting, based on what is in the black box, and thus needs to be dealt with.

As a part of this process, and understanding that which holds you back, my first suggestion would be to pay attention to the ways in which you sabotage yourself. You do so because change is scary, and when changing you will have to get into that place, the black box, and face the contents.

Your defense mechanisms are designed to shield you from emotions that can hurt you. They appear in symptomatic ways and can also sometimes cause you to sabotage good things that are happening to you. In doing so, they are just doing their job, protecting you. These good things, will in time make you face what is in the black box, for in order for them to stay they must be supported on a foundation of positive beliefs. Thus the sabotage is the method by which your defense mechanisms express themselves. Understanding the way in which you sabotage yourself will in turn lead to understanding the limiting belief behind it.

A perfect example of this type of sabotage is this: take a woman who is a mother with a career and she is trying to change and develop herself. When great ideas are brought to her attention she acknowledges that they are good ideas and would help her grow personally as well as her career, and yet she does not embrace these ideas — due to her self-sabotage. She says, "When my kids have graduated then I will..." In truth she is not allowing herself to grow/change, and perhaps she is afraid there is a deeper root cause, but without a doubt she is holding herself back.

It is important to recognize that we all have different modes of sabotage, and each person exhibits it in different ways. The main point is to acknowledge what your methods are and use the different tools in this book to change them, whether you do so with associations, affirmations or visualizations. Recognizing limiting behaviors immediately begins to remove the power that they once had over you.

Now as you read further and see the examples, a part of you may be rejecting this information, and rightly so, this is after all your defense mechanisms at work. I think it is worth noting that most of the behaviors that you exhibit, limiting or otherwise, are all on an unconscious level, so rest assured you are not being accused here in any way. I am simply opening the door for you to peek through. The next step is undoubtedly yours.

Physically, the neurons in our brains are connected, also based on our associations and understandings of the world around us. Once again I think that it is imperative to point out that the less you make the same associations (the old ones) the less they physically become connected, as well as psychologically connected. As a result they lose their connectivity and over time you will notice the new associations are now in place. It only takes one moment to change an association, for it to lose its strength, and for change to take place. But as long as you continue to think in the new way, the neurons in your brain will continue to fire in the new sequence, replacing the old pattern.

Knowing that change can come as easily and as simply as changing your approach just one time is phenomenal, and proves the elasticity of your mind, and its ability to create for you, so that you can become what you want to be.

Once you know what holds you back and how, you can be rid of the old noose and begin to create new and exciting associations with the world and people around you.

Remember the only thing to fear, is fear itself!

CHAPTER SUMMARY

- Ø You need to effect change in your external behavior, as well as your internal thoughts.
- Ø No matter what, you will always project the mental concept of yourself.
- Ø The contents of your black box dictate the way you engage with the world.
- Ø The contents of your black box are negative and need to be resolved.
- Ø Self-sabotage is a product of the black box.
- Ø The less you make old, limiting associations, the less physically and psychologically-connected they become.
- Ø You only need to change an association or belief once, for it to lose strength and new associations to be accepted.

4
Feelings & Intentions

In the last few chapters we spent a lot of time discovering more about the mind, and how it works. It is good to retain this information, as it will help you understand what is holding you back from achieving your goals.

It is also imperative to note that most of our models of the world and concepts have come from our parents and their understanding of the world. As they have grown and learnt, in part due to trial and error, they in turn learned from their life lessons and passed this on to you. It is, once again, your choice of which models you want to keep, and continue to live by, knowing that these models are the basis from which you understand and relate to the world around you.

Regardless of how many non-useful or negative models

you throw away, it is important to understand that the point is not to lay blame at the feet of your parents, but to understand that they have done their best in providing you with the knowledge you have. Similarly, their parents did their best and so on and so forth. Just as you are learning to grow and change, so did they. The difference is simply this; you have available to you a wealth of knowledge that generations past did not have access to. As a result of this, change is certainly easier, (and also more welcome), in this day and age.

In this chapter, and the next few chapters, the focus is now more on the change process and the "how to" of most tools. How to implement them and make them work for you, and understanding the concepts as a whole.

As mentioned earlier, the universe that we live in is based on feelings. The universe responds to feelings. And it is what you feel, more than what you think, that guides your desires and ultimately what you attract into your life.

However, if you do not give your mind a positive picture from which to generate feelings, you may create a negative picture, and this will then create a negative feeling. As a result, you will have once again attracted what you don't want. When you have a picture in your mind, the feelings associated with that picture are what allow you to successfully attract that particular thing.

Let's take an example. It is common for most people to think of the beach as a place of relaxation. When you visualize yourself sitting on the beach on a beautiful island tanning, certain emotions are elicited within you. These emotions become magnified, in turn you attract the idea, the reality of you sitting on the beach. The universe receives your impression of what it is like to be on the beach: the picture and feeling of you there, relaxed, calm and at peace. The universe then responds to this feeling of relaxation and in response you find yourself making plans to go to the beach, and cosmically everything comes into alignment for you to do this.

Now, this is how "like attracts like" operates. If you feel irritated most days and are often agitated, naturally you attract more things that will make you feel even more irritated. This is a cycle and can become one of positivity or one of negativity, depending on what you *choose* to see.

I emphasize the word choose, as again whether or not you realize it, you always have a choice in what you are feeling, and therefore attracting. Knowing that if you remain positive, you will attract more positive things, it is vital that you stay in a positive state of mind as often as you can, for as long as you can.

Now I know to stay in such a state is not easy. However, you have been habituated into the way you think and so it only takes a bit of time, and new habits, to adopt another form of thinking. A great way to stay with a preferred state of mind is to anchor yourself emotionally. An anchor is a useful tool; no matter how far you go, it will bring you back to the point that you want to come to. In this case the point of return is feeling good. The anchor has to be something, or someone, that is a constant in your life, that can make you feel good instantaneously — like a favorite song, or a pet, or a baby. The possibilities are endless. I encourage you to create a list of a few of these anchors, and keep them near, so that you remain in this state as often as possible.

We have established that when you feel good you attract more good things. Now, what most people do not know is that when you continue to remain in this state you tend to attract things that you don't even realize you are attracting; more good things. Things naturally fall into place and automatically align themselves to work in your favor. If you are feeling good and maintain that, but forget to visualize the parking spot you want, chances are it will be there anyway, just as a new client or an unexpected gift may appear.

The Law of Attraction works in the same way. As you feel good, and attract something, as you remain in this state, the universe sends you more good things of the same type. And like all things positive, this principle works for the negative too. If you are in a negative state and you continue to feel this way without 're-calibrating' yourself, you are in turn attracting more of the same type of negative things. For instance, you attract a parking ticket, you do not re-calibrate and now you attract a speeding ticket. To re-calibrate you just take a moment and reflect on the negative feelings you have, then use one of your anchors to make it positive, and turn it around.

Now I know most of you are now asking this question: "If you re-calibrate even after being negative for a couple of hours, how do you know that the negativity of those hours is not still there waiting for you?" The good news is that a positive thought is hundreds of times more powerful than a negative thought, and in re-calibrating you have pretty much reversed the effects of the negative vibrations.

However, I know for some this is not enough, and many times for me it has not been. To make this more effective you can take the re-calibration one step further and re-calibrate the seed of the situation. For instance, you had an argument with someone and lost your temper. In most cases you often realize with hindsight that you could have responded to a situation more appropriately. You realize, once you are calm, how negative you were and you wish to change this. Go back to the time of the argument. Now at the initial point where you reacted to the other person, instead see yourself reacting differently, perhaps more calm. This now re-calibrates the seed.

It is important to re-calibrate the past before you re-calibrate the present, in order to avoid exacerbating any problems in the present.

Your intent is another facet that guides your behavior, and therefore what you attract to you. You get back what you give. If you are prepared to give nothing, regardless of the situation, you will in turn get back the very same thing, nothing. Let's take an example of this.

It is common, when you are fighting with someone that you intend to speak with them in the hopes that by telling them off you are going to get an apology. Surely this will not happen, for you went into this situation giving nothing yet expecting something in return, and as a law this does not work. However, if you went in with only the intent of sharing how you feel, you would get back more than you put in, and certainly more than you can imagine.

The key here is your intent. Your intent is a huge part of what guides behavior and in turn accounts for change. Your intentions are pure only when they are allowed to work for you, and manifest without question or sabotage from the creator, you. Again, this focuses on the importance of letting go and having faith in the process and the outcome. If you want something to manifest, what most people do not know is by intending it you automatically visualize it and in turn begin to manifest it.

A fabulous way to manifest, using your intent, is to create a vacuum. The universe abhors a vacuum and in creating a vacuum you are creating a space that will be filled with what you want/need, by the universe. In order to create a vacuum you must commit to an action which creates an empty space – creating room for something else. Once you have created this space, for example, doing something you have been meaning to do to clear some space, such as clean out your closet, you then command the universe to fill this new empty space what you now want, for instance, more money. You clean out your closet, and in return the universe sends you more prosperity.

Now you are commanding the universe to fill the empty space, through your intent. This command can be in the form of a simple action. However, it is your intent, which will guide it. For instance: "I will weed the garden, and in return the universe will send me more prosperity."

You have created a vacuum using your intent, by doing something that creates a space which was not there before and commanding something in return. At this point, because you have created the vacuum, know that this is your intent and reason for getting out of bed that day. Completing a task creates a vacuum and in completing this said task a space has been created. It is in this space that, by your intent that you are filling with that which you want.

Your feelings are very important, just as your visualizations are. Although the feelings you generate are for the universe to understand what you are creating, the picture in your mind serves its purpose too. As mentioned earlier, the human mind is created as a goal-striving mechanism. In the absence of a goal, if it is predominantly negative, the mind will create a negative goal, and once again you will find yourself in a place where you do not want to be, although you did create it.

If when visualizing you are unable to feel what it would be like for that specific thing to be your reality, in truth you have not accomplished anything.

Once you have created, whether by simply intending something or visualizing it, the next step is to project it. It is vital to note that humans consistently project thoughts and images into the world, whether they know it or not. When you project what you feel, you are attracting, and physically manifesting whatever you have created in your mind.

When you project your thoughts and feelings you do so without effort. A projection requires no effort. It simply is the energy that you radiate outwards, that is felt by all. You first hold the thought of your goal, for example a million dollars in your mind, knowing that it is yours, feeling as though you already have it, and seeing the picture of what a million dollars means to you. Through your confidence you transmit the idea that you have a million dollars, and in turn the universe brings it to you.

The reason that projection is mentioned is to explain it fully. It is in fact something that happens naturally. As long as you are working through the issues that hold you back, and staying positive and focused on your goals, you are, and will be, projecting good energy. You project what you feel, always, and so when you feel good and remain in this state consistently, you automatically are projecting that. Focus on your positive feelings and thoughts, the rest will fall into place.

CHAPTER SUMMARY

- Ø You choose the models of the world to guide you, and create the world that you want to live in.
- Ø The universe responds to feelings.
- Ø Like attracts like.
- Ø You can choose what you feel and therefore what you attract into your life.
- Ø Emotional anchors help you stay in a positive frame of mind.
- Ø A positive thought is hundreds of times more powerful than a negative thought.
- Ø Your intentions also affect what you attract into your life.

5

Visualization

During the course of this book we have spent a great deal of time using the word visualization and acknowledging this as a very effective method to achieve your goals. On some level we all know how to visualize and what it means to visualize. However, to use this process effectively, it is important to cover the basics, to ensure that you are completely successful in creating what you want.

Visualizing is seeing a picture in your mind's eye and instructing your mind to follow through and make that image a reality. As you already know, the mind does not know the difference between what is real or imagined, nor what is perceived to be negative or positive. What you see in your mind, you create in your life; in essence this is how you use the Law of Attraction.

You have been visualizing for many years, whether you

realize it or not. It is common, when you think about the route you will take home from work, or to the grocery store, automatically you see a picture in your mind of the route, thereby instructing your subconscious mind to follow the best roads to get there. Similarly, if you chose to avoid that route, but still saw that same route in your mind, you would find yourself on that road wondering how on earth you got there, when you had decided not to take that specific route.

Remember, the mind sees in pictures, and uses these to focus on goals. Saying "no" to a picture whilst you see it only reinforces that picture and does not in fact negate it. In order to say "no" to something, or in this case take a different route home, you would have to show your mind, in a picture, another route as opposed to simply saying "no". Again this is also because the mind does not know the difference between a positive or a negative event. Your mind is designed to fulfill the goals you give it. It is not designed to censor what is good or bad for you. That is what your emotions are there for.

Another example of this is what we mentioned in Chapter One: the child who said he did not want to be his father but in his mind saw himself becoming exactly like his father. Even though he said it was something he did not want, in seeing the picture in his mind he sent the instruction to his mind, and this is why he finds years later he has become just like his father.

So how do you visualize? It is important to think in detail, and to do so daily, making a habit out of it. If thinking negatively is a habit then so can visualizing and thinking positive become a habit. The more details you see: colors, textures, shapes, physical environment, people – size, physical appearance, facial expressions, body movement, etc., the clearer the instruction you are sending to your subconscious, making the execution of the plan faster, and exactly what you want, based on what you visualized.

One of my favorite analogies perfectly illustrates this. It is from 'Psycho-Cybernetics' by Maxwell Maltz. In this book he likens the mechanisms of the mind to that of a missile. He states that the mind is like a missile and it has a target, the goal. The visualizations are the coordinates that are used to guide the missile. The better the visualizations, the more specific the coordinates are, ensuring the target is successfully reached.

A really great way of visualizing, that is powerful and effective, is to imagine that you are in a movie theatre. See yourself sitting in the theatre and watching a movie. However, the movie that is playing is the visualization you want to see. This will allow you to visualize more precisely and not get distracted when you are starting out.

The next essential step to visualizing is to only see the end goal. Many people are often in the process of looking for a job. If you are in the process of looking for a job, then now is the time to use this skill. It is vital for you to only see the end result, which in this case is the job itself. Now I know it is hard to imagine the end result, especially if you do not know where you are going to be working.

However, it is imperative that you decide upon what that looks like. In this case it could be the vision of you going to work, or coming home from work. You see yourself feeling good, relaxed, and proud of the productive day you have had. You want to see what having the job actually looks like for you. Are you in an office, working from home, or somewhere else? Having that job may also mean the option to go out for dinner more often, to travel, or to go to the movies. Whatever it may be, that is what you need to focus on.

When you visualize the method by which you want to achieve that goal, you are in essence telling the universe that the only way in which you can get this job, as in the above example, is through this particular method. Now, in order for all the variables to fit and for all the right energies to line up in order for you to get this job, it may take months or years. However, if you let go of the method and focus on the end result you are acknowledging that you do not care how getting the job comes about, only that it does.

A great example of this is money. Most people want a million dollar lifestyle. If you visualized having millions of dollars, then I am certain you do not care where or how you get the money. Our natural tendency is to lean towards the lottery, however if you visualized the lottery you could potentially wait for years for this to happen, as so many recipients are wanting to tap into just that one source!

Now, if you just state that it is money you want, it will come to you regardless of how. You could perhaps inherit it, someone could gift it to you, and you certainly could win the lottery. The point is that in telling the universe how you want something to come about, is only limiting you, for there is no way that you can imagine all the possibilities for it to happen for you.

Once you have visualized that which you want, or rather the end goal of it, the next thing to do is attach feelings or emotions to this picture. At first you will find you are visualizing and then generating the feeling. These will quickly merge however, and you will find that you are simultaneously visualizing and feeling. Without the feeling you have not done anything. The associated feeling tells the universe what you want.

Your life today is the product of your past visualizations, and in turn, your visualizations today will shape the tomorrow that you are looking for. Another effective method to make certain your visualizations are effective is to do them in the immediate past.

If what you saw yesterday created your experience today, then what you see today creates your tomorrow. However, if when visualizing you go to the immediate past, then you will see the results now.

Let's take an example of this. I often go to the grocery store closest to my house, where parking is a valued commodity that is charged for. There is also a dollar minimum of shopping that you have to do. As I entered the parking lot I pushed the button, retrieved my ticket and proceeded inside the store. As I did so I saw myself entering the parking lot and visualized the parking slip being validated.

By going back to a positive event in the immediate past, the same positive results can come to fruition in the present for another goal; this is also applicable to the near or distant future.

Whether you know it or not, the human mind always goes to the immediate past when visualizing. Using the technique in this way ensures the results are again more favorable for you.

Many times I have been asked if in going back to the past the incidents have to be related, such as in the example above. The answer is that they do not. In fact I could have seen myself as I was getting out of bed that morning and then fast-forwarded to my parking ticket being validated. The key is to go back into the past and then move to the end result of what you want to see. As long as you have gone into the immediate past, it is irrelevant how far or to what event, just ensure you have gone back first, before visualizing for the future.

The more you use the technique of visualizing and become proficient at it, the more it dominos in your life and changes your roots, making them more positive. If your roots become more positive, then your beliefs follow, and in turn you are more likely to visualize positively.

That is not to say that the visualizations you have done to-date are all negative. I am simply pointing out the propensity for most humans to lean towards the negative as the products of their environment. However, if you are already in a positive state then most certainly these techniques will support you, by helping to maintain a predominantly positive mind.

Now, once you have visualized going into the immediate past first, then to bring this scene to the point of projecting it, the next step is to see yourself doing any one thing, utilizing this knowledge. Let's take an example: you have visualized yourself receiving millions of dollars. Once you have completed this step you see yourself grocery shopping, or answering the phone.

The point is this, knowing you have all this money changes the way in which you walk around a grocery store and certainly how you would answer the phone. You would probably be more relaxed and confident. By completing this step you are projecting that you already have this. When you project that you already have something, the universe sends you more. When you have this money you don't care if you win the lottery or not, so you are more likely to win now, because you do not care. This allows what you have visualized to come into being faster.

I know this is quite involved, so before we continue, I will sum this up.

> Step One: Go to the immediate past, even a minute prior
>
> Step Two: Move to the end goal of what you want to happen or receive
>
> Step Three: Find the feelings associated with this (e.g. if it was money you might feel relieved, relaxed, excited and free)
>
> Step Four: See yourself doing any one thing, such as answering the phone, and feeling these emotions
>
> Step Five: Let it go
>
> Immediate Past → End Goal → Attach feelings → Do any task → Know you already have it → Let it go

Follow the above five steps and you will start to see the changes in your life unfold.

A great way to make a habit of visualizing and incorporate it into your daily routine is to take a couple of minutes every morning to visualize your day and how you want it to play out. If you have meetings or presentations, it is imperative that you see the end goal of these events and the outcome you desire.

If there is one particular thing that you want to create, for example getting a new car, take a few minutes daily, visualize having the car, and from different angles. Using the example of the movie theater, imagine the camera is filming from the roof, from outside a window, from the doorway. Seeing things from different angles allows your brain to commit it to memory. Once it becomes a memory it is constantly projected and the brain sees this as reality. Once it becomes a memory, it has in fact already started to come to you and that car will soon be yours. The universe will now complete the last step, of delivering the car to you.

What you say, and the words you choose to express yourself, determine the pictures that your mind creates. For instance, the color red to some may represent a favorite shirt, or a particular food from childhood. When that person says the word "red" in their mind, they see the associated item, and this then immediately becomes a command.

If it is a negative association and a new picture is not substituted, they have commanded this very thing to become reality, such as an injury. Similarly, if it is positive they may find they wear red, or receive a bouquet of red flowers. Thus, it is important to pay attention to the words and their associations, and pictures they create for you, so that you are not, by default, attracting things that you do not want.

The above phenomenon is known as "the power of words". To use this effectively, find an affirmation for a goal that you want to achieve. For example, "I easily attract all the money I need," or "I attract 2 new clients a week," or "I constantly project abundance and prosperity." Each time you state the affirmation, intentionally visualize the goal you want to achieve at the same time. This will also allow you to use the power of your words as a creative mechanism.

Remember, if ever you find yourself visualizing or creating a picture that is negative and one that you do not want, do not shout "no" at it, for your resistant feelings will only bring it to you faster. Instead, re-write the program. In other words, see what you want and focus on that, rather than focusing on what you don't want. Replace the picture, and this will move you in the right direction.

I have often been asked why some visualizations materialize faster than others. Aside from letting go, and creating the feeling associated with the vision there is one other mechanism at play here. In most cases, money takes longer to manifest. If you are holding onto a particular vision of money and it is taking a long time to materialize, it is because you are challenging a limiting belief at the same time as creating a new picture in your mind.

Many people have a voice in their head. This voice that attempts to dissuade you also needs to be quieted, as your mind needs to get used to the concept of having more money. Recognize that there may be more foundational beliefs that need to be challenged on an ongoing basis. Again, take one at a time and this will domino. Hold on to your goal. You will eventually see the fruits of your labor.

I have also been asked why, after a particular goal is created, you are unable to follow through with it. Lack of exercise is a common issue for many individuals today. For instance, you know you need to spend more time being physically active. You know you should work out and so decide to go to the gym. Yet more often than not you cannot commit to this, and find that after a small burst of commitment you are not attending the gym again. (Some don't even have that initial burst.)

If you have this disconnection between what you want and completing it, you have not created a picture that your brain can associate with. Perhaps going to the gym does not really appeal to you and another form of exercise would be better, such as dancing. First, you need to create a picture of what being physically fit means to you, and what you see yourself doing. It may be walking daily, running, exercise classes, dancing, or even yoga. Find the exercise that works for you; one that creates the right association in your mind. Then you will invariably see how quickly you commit to your goals and see them realized.

I recognize this is a great deal of information, and that putting it to use can certainly be overwhelming. I encourage you to embrace this process, but to also have fun with this. The more you practice, the better you will become at it. So have fun, as this is your life!

CHAPTER SUMMARY

- Ø Visualizing is seeing a picture in your mind's eye of what you want.
- Ø Your mind is created to fulfill goals, based on the pictures you provide it with.
- Ø If you are holding onto a picture you do not want in your mind, simply replace it with a picture of what you do want. Do not shout "no", as you just attract more "not having".
- Ø Thinking positive can become a habit.
- Ø Your mind is a goal-striving mechanism.
- Ø Only visualize the end result of what you want.
- Ø When visualizing a goal, you must put it into context, by association, in order for your mind to understand it.
- Ø Attach feelings to your visualizations.
- Ø Visualize in the immediate past to see results now.
- Ø Immediate Past → End Goal → Attach feelings → Do any task → Know you already have it → Let it go.
- Ø Visualize daily and see the picture from different angles to create a new memory.
- Ø The words you choose also create pictures in your mind. Pay attention to these associations.
- Ø If a goal takes longer than expected, it is simply your mind becoming accustomed to the new concept.
- Ø Disconnection between a goal and its manifestation is the result of the brain not receiving associations related to the goal.

6

Letting Go

In previous chapters I have mentioned the concept of letting go. Knowing the difficulties I faced with this concept at one point, I wanted to elaborate on this and how it works. Many clients have also asked me what it is, and how one does it.

Letting go involves not waiting for whatever you have created in your mind to materialize, but knowing that it will come. Letting go is forgetting about whatever you have visualized and going with the flow of your life – i.e. letting things in life take their natural course, and not pushing against things that are not falling into place. And just as you need to let go after visualizing, you also need to let go of your old concepts and ideas to allow the new ones to come forth.

Here is an example of letting go that my teacher provided; it truly resonated with me and helped me to grasp this concept more fully.

It is first thing in the morning and you are in the kitchen making breakfast. You put your spoon down on the counter to tend to something else. You come back, and yet for the life of you, you cannot find the spoon. You search all the counter tops and even begin looking in other places, thinking you may have taken it with you and unknowingly placed it elsewhere. You come back to the kitchen, not having found the spoon. At this point, without caring, you go to the drawer for another one. As soon as you do, the spoon that you could not originally see materializes before you. The reason you now see the original one is because you no longer cared about it, and went to get another spoon - you let go of it.

I am sure you can think back to many occasions in your life where you have let go, without doing it consciously. Once you have visualized what you want, if you do not let go, this visualization will not come into being. Questioning it, waiting for it, wondering why it has not happened yet, are all ways of holding on. When you participate in this kind of thinking you are in fact sabotaging whatever you have visualized, and can affect the outcome. It only takes a moment to let go, and in that instant it starts to come to you.

Let's take an example of this. For many people selling a house is an emotional and eventful occasion. I have a friend who was selling her house. She wanted desperately to see this happen and so I coached her and helped her visualize the sale of the house and the price that she wanted for it. Once we did this the next step for her was to let it go. Unable to do so, she was plagued with the fear of not selling, and really needed the money. She was so consumed by this she literally could not let go. Having advised her on several occasions that she was the only one holding herself back, at some point this obviously registered. One month later she let go, and it took only a second. For the second she let go, in that same moment a call came from the real estate agent informing her that she had an offer. However, as a result of her not being able to let go earlier, although she had an offer it was not for the price that she initially intended. Her questions and her anxiety changed the outcome.

To use the analogy of the missile from the previous chapter, negative thoughts you may experience after a visualization only act to change the coordinates of the missile you have sent out. So you may still hit your target, but it may not be a bull's eye!

Now, how do you know that you have let go? The universe works really fast; in fact the instant you let go your visualization is manifested. Although, there is another facet of this; it is already created but you may not be in the right frequency yet to receive it, or it may not be the right time for you to see it.

That does not mean you have not let go. For example, numerous people when traveling are particular about their accommodations. You have an upcoming vacation and you have determined that you want to stay in a particular hotel but have been told as this is a group trip that will be decided upon your arrival. You have seen the hotel options and selected the one you would like. You have also visualized the one you want. Once you have let go, this visualization has come to fruition. However, you cannot see the results until you get to your destination.

First, you need to be in the right frequency. Look at the example of the young lady selling her house. Had she let go, and stayed positive she would have seen her house sell much quicker. The reason it did not was due to the fact that she was feeling so negative that she was not at the right frequency to see it happen. Once she relaxed and allowed it to happen, it did so. She rejected the first offer, but quickly received another, when she finally let go.

The secret to letting go is to get on with something else. I too have had my troubles with letting go and sometimes it has been hard. Thankfully I am long past that and you too will get to this point. The secret is to simply move on. When you have tasks to attend to, you do so. Don't dwell on it once it is done. Countless people complete a household chore and move on. Just as when you complete this household chore such as the dishes, you unload the dishes from the dishwasher and then get on with something else. You don't think about it or dwell on how you unloaded the dishes.

Once you have visualized what you want, don't tell yourself you are not going to think about it. Simply banish it from your mind and move on. Remember, you can and will think of the things that you have visualized. That is normal. The key is to let go each time. So, you can think of it a million times; as long as you let go a million times, it will not change the outcome. In this way visualize what you want and then forget about it, knowing it is done, and get on with work or whatever you are doing. Don't tell yourself not to think about it, remember the mind does not know the difference between "do" and "don't". Either get on with something else and keep doing that, or think about it, but keep letting it go.

This is something that takes practice and honestly you just have to keep doing it. As for the questions that come after, they do come for everyone and certainly make you doubt. Differentiate between the old you and the new one. When the doubts come, acknowledge them. My favorite way to deal with them is to say, "Thank you. You should stick around because you remind me of where I have come from." Once I have said this they go away instantly.

Remember, the old you is trying to stop you from growing, the defense mechanisms think they are protecting you. Your mechanisms mean well, but when you ignore them they get louder. When you acknowledge them, they disappear, as all they want is to be heard.

To let go is not to expect. If you expect that which you have created to happen, you will be disappointed, as it will not come. It will come when you have truly forgotten and gone on with your day and not waiting for that very thing to appear.

When you let go, you don't care if that visualization materializes or not because you know, on another level that everything will work out perfectly. When you are at this point, the universe sends more your way. When you don't need more, the universe sends you more. You were created with a mind that works best when relaxed and not stressed. With a stressed mind you cannot create. When you worry, you are telling the universe that you don't believe your visualization will come true, and the universe then does not manifest, because you do not believe.

Let's take an example of getting more when you don't care. Take the example of a man who has a heart condition, he plays the lottery and wins $100,000. He knows that his time is limited, yet he is so happy with what he has, he does not care about anything. He feels free, relaxed and calm. In this mode, if you asked him to play the lottery again he would probably win again. Because he does not care. He is happy with that which he has and if he were to get more it would not matter.

Letting go is knowing that you have options and so you are not focused on any one outcome, and all outcomes will bring you the result that you want, as you have visualized the end goal.

When you create your success, let go, as you did that spoon you were temporarily unable to find. Continue on your path and know, that your success, like the spoon, will appear when you least expect it.

CHAPTER SUMMARY

- Ø Letting go is knowing and not expecting.
- Ø It only takes a second to let go.
- Ø Once you have completed a visualization, get on with another task. This will facilitate letting go.
- Ø A distinction between the old you vs. the new you will allow you to let go even more.
- Ø Letting go is not caring about the outcome, as you have options.

7

Negative Self Talk

Throughout this book we have discussed the concept of change and the process of it. I have mentioned the negative thoughts that we all experience as a result of change as well as the old mechanisms that attempt to prevent change.

Many of my clients have often shared with me the frustrations they feel through the change process, most especially as a result of the resistance that the mind provides during this. Negative thoughts, doubts and feelings of uncertainty are normal during change, and we all have experienced them at one time or another. It is however imperative that you ignore the ways in which your mind creates resistance, in order to carry on and succeed with this process.

Your defense mechanisms are working very hard at the moment to dissuade you from change. It is important to recognize that they are trying to protect you and the more you understand these mechanisms and what they are protecting you from, the sooner you are able to resolve these issues and move forward.

We have talked about the other voice in your head. This voice is the way your mechanisms converse with you and guide you. At times, this voice can be very harsh and discouraging. Acknowledge what it has to say and move on. By recognizing its goal, to protect you, and by acknowledging the old you and the new you, you are creating a distinctive boundary in order to facilitate change.

The new you no longer has to listen to that voice. The new you is positive and pro-active and not hindered by anything. This expanded way of thinking allows change to occur more rapidly.

It is important to note that once you have resolved your issues, and you will over time, the defense mechanisms and the voice no longer need to be there, and disappear. At this point the old and new you can now merge as change has occurred at the root level. Not only are you feeling and thinking positively on the conscious level; but on a subconscious level as well. As you continue to challenge your ways of thinking and maintain the new models of behavior there will no longer become any need for a black box or defense mechanisms. This happens naturally and you will simply notice this one day. The voice associated with the new you will now be consistently encouraging and supportive.

As with all things in life, there are cycles. Change too works in a cycle and there are ups and downs. This is part of the learning curve and everyone has to go through this change. The great part about this type of change is this, once the human brain has been through a transformation, such as the one we have been focusing on, it will always retain some level of positivity and will never return to its old habits and ways of thinking. Furthermore, the ups last longer than the downs.

Let's make a distinction between these two polarities. When I refer to up, I mean the state of mind you are in when you are feeling positive, focused, excited and energized. Alternatively, down is when you are feeling negative and unconstructive.

The down is when you are feeling your most pessimistic, or lost. The good news is that once your brain feels the change of a positive state just once, it will never return to the same low, ever again. Your ups will get higher, but so will your downs. Eventually your down will perhaps be a neutral state and not even a negative one. So although there may be this feeling of going back and forth for a period of time, and though you may dread the downs, embrace them, knowing that you will certainly be going up again. By rejoicing during the times when you are feeling down, you allow your other experiences to be much more positive.

Using these techniques, you will notice how often you will be in an 'up' state, and how this state of mind is addictive. As a part of this process, making the distinction between the old you versus the new you, is critical for successful change and also acceptance of change by your mind.

SELF-SABOTAGING PATTERNS

Self sabotage includes situations when you get a "bad feeling" about someone or something. Remember, when an incident or a person causes an emotional reaction within you, especially a negative emotional response, it is always about you. Let me explain. The feelings that a person or situation raise in you could be a result of you not wanting to recognize the same feeling within you, perhaps jealousy, or having been in a similar situation and been hurt. Thus, the bad feeling is only protecting you from thinking about why person A "rubs you the wrong" way and perhaps digging deeper to find the cause and resolving it. Your brain is protecting you because digging for this resolve is not an easy process and is more often than not a painful one.

There will be times where, as a result of turning your attention inwards, emotions can be overwhelming. On many a day you may find that you are at a loss over how to cope with this, feeling that you do not have the ability. Although there is a list of helpful exercises mentioned in this book, the support of a therapist, counselor or coach at this point is crucial to passing through the tunnel of emotions. I encourage you to seek out this help, if you have not done so already, as a support.

A great way to combat the emotional overwhelm is to complete what I call the "Fact-Emotion Technique". This technique helps you to pinpoint your emotions, as you separate them from the facts. In doing so the facts not only become clearer, the emotions loosen their hold on you, and certainly make moving forward easier. Let me give you an example. You wake up in the morning and stub your toe at the foot of your bed, cursing and muttering under your breath and feeling irritable, angry that you stubbed your toe. You now see the rest of your day being a bad one, because when you stubbed your toe you automatically visualized all this.

The fact is that you stubbed your toe; it made you angry and so the consequence of that emotion is now the belief that you are having a bad day. If you were able to look at the situation from a factual point of view you would be able to isolate the anger from the stubbing of the toe. When you stubbed your toe, you cursed, but also resolved your irritability, and stated that you were going to have a good day. Your emotion, anger, which was not resolved, led you to believe that your day would be a negative one. And so it was.

Many clients mention confusion between working through emotions, especially when they are negative, and staying positive. For a while you will continue to experience negative emotions. Remember, you are working through your emotional history and so you are bound to have some pain. Recognizing and working through your less desirable experiences is important. However, the feelings you emerge from this process with are even more important.

When you have cried and feel that you have been negative, once you move into a positive state and can find something to be positive about, you have grown; this is what you take away with you. The positive feelings. When you can be glad for the down moments because you are grateful for learning more about you, you will attract more learning about you, and that can only be a good thing. So focus on what positive feelings each situation gives you; this will help you employ this Law to the fullest.

I am certain that as you open your black box you will find other ways in which you have been sabotaging yourself and did not even know it. And I am even more sure, that you will find other tools as you go on your journey to resolve these issues that hold you back. Continue to add more tools to your collection, as you will soon find that many along the way, and all may come in handy.

I encourage you to simply acknowledge the negative aspects of this process and move on. Do not allow them to plague you, for they will, in time disappear.

Happy Visualizing!

CHAPTER SUMMARY

- Ø Doubts and negative thoughts are normal during the change process.
- Ø Acknowledge the voice in your head, it will quieten.
- Ø Once you incorporate positivity into your life, you will always retain some degree of it.
- Ø Your highs become higher and your lows become higher when you remain focused.
- Ø When feeling down, rejoice in this knowing you are attracting what you want, and you will soon feel up again.
- Ø Any emotional response you have to the world around you, is always about you. Your emotions are being triggered. Choose your responses.
- Ø Separate your emotions from a situation, then you can deal with the facts.
- Ø Turn negative emotions into a positive state of learning.

Conclusion

The Law of Attraction is always working, and if used properly, is designed to give you everything that you want. Using it intentionally and applying the use of feelings will ensure that you are receiving whatever you want.

As you re-read this book, and perhaps research new concepts learned here, you will begin to understand your conscious and subconscious: how they work for you and how they hamper you. Remember, your mind does not know the difference between something that is visualized versus something that is real. As you become more comfortable with this concept, change will become easier. It is essential that you keep your attention on what you want, rather than on what you do not want.

Your beliefs are a choice, once you recognize that they do not have to limit you, you will be surprised at how easy they are to let go of. Once you have let go, you will be able to create an alignment between your conscious mind and your subconscious mind. When you stop engaging with unwanted beliefs, they lose their power over you.

The contents of the black box need to be exorcised; the more it opens, the more free you are of old patterns of thought. Your defenses keep this box operational, yet through these defense mechanisms you begin to understand your limiting thoughts, as well as the ways in which you sabotage yourself.

Remember, you function in a universe that is based on feelings. Your mind receives information in the form of pictures, once you attach an emotion to a picture you are in fact creating. Anchoring yourself, re-calibration, and filling a vacuum, are a few ways in which to use your mind and emotions, in order to manifest what you want.

A visualization is seeing a picture in your mind's eye. If you use the 5-step process covered in this book, it will help you to become more efficient and successful in this skill and make it a habitual part of you. Remember to pay attention to the words you use, for they too create pictures and in turn contribute to the life you are designing.

As you continue on with the creative process, reflect on the concept of letting go. Keep your expectations in check and live in the now. How frequently you visualize will effect how soon you will see results. In other words, the level at which the cells of your body are vibrating, and the amount of positive energy they are exuding will dictate these results. Move on to something else, and automatically you will let go.

Finally, note that the negative internal voice that at times plagues you, will eventually disappear, and is just a part of the initial change process.

I hope this knowledge helps you find your bliss. The purpose of this book is to be a guide, a system for successful change, whilst making the process fun, exciting and certainly challenging. May you find courage in your process and new hope for all your dreams of today and tomorrow.

I would love to hear your thoughts on your journey and welcome e-mails from you. I can be reached at **muneeza.khimji@gmail.com**

Good luck! I know you will fulfill your dreams, using the techniques in this book, just as I have done and continue to do so.

CHAPTER SUMMARY

- Understand your conscious and subconscious mind and the ways in which they hinder or help you.
- Keep your attention on what you want.
- Understand the ways in which you limit yourself.
- Know you live in a universe that is based on feelings.
- Realize that your mind views information in the form of pictures.
- Make visualizing a habit.
- Keep your expectations in check .
- Allow yourself to flow.
- Use the exercises frequently. Add more, as you see what works for you.

METHODS OF LEARNING

These exercises are provided to help you through your journey of change. Some of these will work for you and some may not. I encourage you to use those that do and tweak those that don't, to suit your needs.

1. LIST OF BELIEFS

By making a list of beliefs, or the models by which you operate, you are able to identify and choose the ones you want to keep versus those that were given to you, that you no longer want. This exercise gives you an idea of what you want to change and why you are choosing different frameworks by which to live your life.

2. CHANGE RESPONSE TO YOUR ENVIRONMENT

Most of us respond with agitation and irritation to the stressors in our environment. When you change the way you respond, i.e., by being calm and relaxed, you change what you are attracting.

3. ANCHORING EMOTIONALLY

This is a good way to always keep focused on feeling good and remaining in a frequency that reflects that. A song, a particular person, a pet or anything that makes you feel good. Keep this anchor close by and use it when you find you are dipping into a negative vibe to stay in a positive one. Do this as often as you need to.

4. RE-CALIBRATING

When you are slipping into a negative vibration, it is vital that you re-calibrate as soon as possible so you don't attract more negative vibrations. Think of something that makes you happy and brings joy to you. As soon as you can feel the joy, you are re-calibrating. Remember, you can calibrate the seed too by going back to the source of the stress and re-visualizing your response to a particular situation.

5. CREATING A VACUUM

The universe abhors a vacuum and in creating a vacuum you are creating a space, and the universe will fill that space, with what you ask for. You create what you want with your intent. With your intent you are projecting what you want and guiding the universe to bring it to you. In other words if you intend to clean out a drawer, in return for better health, by intending this (saying it and visualizing yourself as healthy) you have in fact manifested by your intent.

6. ALWAYS VISUALIZE END GOAL

Visualizing what you want allows you to create what you want to manifest. What makes a visualization successful is seeing only the end goal; this allows the universe to bring you what you want, regardless of how it needs to do so.

7. MOVIE SCREEN EXERCISE

Imagine you are in a movie theatre. On the screen is what you want to visualize. Watching it play out like a movie allows you to see it in detail, as well as be very specific about what you are seeing. If you have a tough time seeing certain things, such as your physical self, just view details that you can identify, such as a watch, or a scar. This will allow you to visualize with clarity and focus.

8. VISUALIZE YOUR DAY

When you wake up in the morning, get into the habit of taking a couple of minutes to create your day. Remember to keep seeing the end goal only. See exactly how you want your day to be. For example see a successful meeting; the end result of completing a project. Add your feelings, then let this go. As you go about your day you will see it come to fruition perfectly.

9. AFFIRMATIONS AND VISUALIZATIONS

Taking an affirmation to the next level is to repeat your mantra and at the same time see the picture of the association in your mind, for example, stating that you make a lot of money and the association of you traveling first class could indicate what having more money means to you. As you do this you reaffirm to your mind and the universe exactly what you want and what it looks like.

10. ACKNOWLEDGE THE OLD

This is a fabulous way to make the distinction between the old you and new you and a great way to move away from negative voices stopping your progress. Just say, "Thank you. You remind me of where I came from."

11. FACT-EMOTION TECHNIQUE

This is a great way to learn to separate your emotions from a situation in order to not react negatively to it. Determine what the facts are (make a list) and then determine what emotions are contributing to the situation (make a list). This will allow you to objectively deal with situations without becoming negative.

EXTENDED EXERCISES/METHODS

1. OLD NEW VS NEW YOU

When you begin this process of change, making the distinction between the two versions allows you to break free from the beliefs that hold you back. This distinction allows you to change (the new you) and allows the old you to resolve issues, until it can incorporate the new beliefs that you are putting into place.

2. BE TRUTHFUL

Say out loud how you feel, as this makes it less daunting or emotional. If you are embarrassed and don't want to say it to someone else, say it to yourself in private. As long as you acknowledge the fear, or the emotion, out loud, you will not be as overwhelmed.

3. ASK YOUR HIGHER SELF FOR GUIDANCE

We all have a Higher Self (or subconscious) and looking to that part of us for guidance is a great way to receive the answers you are looking for. Before you go to sleep at night ask your Higher Self for guidance or an answer; you will be surprised by the results.

4. VISUALIZE YOURSELF DEVELOPING

You want to see yourself going with the flow, not allowing any incident or circumstance to interrupt your relaxed mode and calm mind. The more you visualize yourself this way, the more often you will flow and be at a frequency to receive all the things you have visualized.

5. MILLION DOLLAR EXERCISE

This is a great exercise to generate and project the attitude of not caring so that more comes your way. Imagine you have a million dollars. How would you feel? How would you walk down the street if you had this much money? How would you answer the phone? Practice having all these feelings and new behaviors, and you will attract a million- dollar-lifestyle, if not a million dollars.

6. BREATHING EXERCISES

At times when we are emotional, feelings of being overwhelmed can come easily and distress you. Breathe in on the count of 3 to 5 seconds, hold for 3 to 5 seconds, and exhale for 3 to 5 seconds. When you hold your breath, imagine your breath is a magnet and all your stress is attracted to it. When you exhale, see the stress leaving your body through your breath. This can be represented by mist, or a color, or whatever else comes to mind.

7. ANCHORING PHYSICALLY

Pick a point on your body that you can access easily, such as your elbow. As you experience moments where you are feeling positive, focused, excited and energized, touch it, and with your intent, transfer the positive energy to this point. Then whenever you are feeling low you can instantly access these good feelings by simply touching your elbow. It is a quick and easy way to bounce back by re-calibrating your feelings.

8. JOURNALING

Words are a powerful way to manifest what you want. Write down what you want to attract, which will give greater focus to your goals. Additionally, this is a great way to look at emotions that you are having trouble coping with.

9. USING EMOTIONS TO FACILITATE CHANGE

Change can be daunting. Our habitual responses tend to perpetuate old emotional cycles. Changing your response to a situation in the moment allows you to break the cycle, and facilitate change on a deeper level.

10. ASSOCIATIONS

You can visualize anything you desire, however it must be placed in a structure that the mind can follow. Since the mind sees in pictures, should you decide to create more money for yourself, you must see what that amount of money means to you. It must relate to the picture of the lifestyle you want, as the brain cannot conceptualize a number only.

11. AFFIRMATIONS

Affirmations are another great way to create. Words can trigger change. They work by repetition of a particular goal, making it the sole focus of the mind. The more affirmations you use, the more successful you are, as the mind does not have the ability to sabotage them when there are too many.

12. FEELING THANKFUL

This is a very important exercise that we should all use as often as we can. The more you appreciate what you have, the more you attract of the same thing. You can even give thanks for what you don't have yet, but want, and the universe will bring it to you. Do this daily as it continues to keep you on a positive path.

GLOSSARY

ABUNDANCE

A state of mind where one knows and experiences an ample supple of everything, and knows there is enough to satisfy the entire world.

AFFIRMATIONS

Words that are powerful in meaning, that when repeated regularly cause a specific change in attitude or belief and are useful to bring about progressive change.

ANCHOR

A physical or emotional device that provides a means of staying stable. It allows one to remain in a positive frame of mind by referring back to it as often as needed.

ASSOCIATIONS

The framework by which the mind understands the goals that are being set out, in the form of pictures and models through which each individual relates to the world.

BLACK BOX

A part of the subconscious mind that houses all negative experiences and associations, including limiting beliefs.

CONSCIOUS MIND

The part of the mind where everyday decisions and thoughts originate from. It is everything one is aware of including some memories. It is the part of the mind that everyone is aware of on a regular basis.

DEFENSE MECHANISMS

These are behaviors that the subconscious mind has developed in response to a perceived threat, real or imagined. They are designed to protect against a threat, and will cause avoidance of situations in order to achieve this.

DISCONNECTION

This is a state of emotions where the mind cannot understand the goal that has been set out, as it has not been put into the context of a familiar framework. As a result there is a lack of a connection between the goal and the picture of the goal.

DOMINO EFFECT

When change takes place in one part of the mind, this causes resultant change in other parts of the mind, as well as behavior. When new ways of response are adopted in any area of life, causing new more expansive experiences, this touches and changes other areas of life simultaneously. Change occurs in exactly the same way as dominos fall - as they are all connected, the movement of any one effects all of them.

DOWN

When one is in an emotional state where feelings of negativity, frustration and irritability are prominent.

FREQUENCY

The vibrational level the cells in the human body are moving at, which dictates the state of mind. The slower the vibration, the calmer and therefore more positive state a person is in.

FRUITION

This is the attainment or realization of something that is visualized.

GOAL-STRIVING MECHANISM

The human mind is designed as a mechanism that when given a picture that in the right context and framework, will fulfill the goal, regardless of whether or not it is positive.

IMMEDIATE PAST

This is the point which becomes a reference for creation in the now. It is used in direct relation to the present in order to see immediate results.

INTENT

The act of turning the mind to a desire with purpose, including creating a picture to achieve a goal.

LAW OF ATTRACTION

The ability to create based on the mode of thinking and feeling. Like attracts like.

LETTING GO

Knowing that things have been put into motion, but not waiting for the results, once a goal has been visualized. Being aware that there are always many options for its manifestation, and being open to whatever comes, and how.

MANIFESTED

When a goal is realized and appears on the physical material plane, it has been manifested.

POWER OF WORDS

When a particular word or phrase is used it creates an association in the mind, a picture, which then becomes a tool for creating what is desired.

PROJECT

Energy that is composed of thoughts, feelings and beliefs is emitted from each individual. Sending out energy from the mind to attract and manifest a goal. As the energy is emitted it magnetizes and draws back the same energy, in the form of people, relationships, jobs, money, material possessions, or events.

RE-CALIBRATE

The ability to reassess a negative situation and with insight know that it needs to be changed. One changes it by thinking of something positive to replace the negative feelings.

ROOT LEVEL

The source where a thought or behavior stems from, and where it was instinctively created. Change at this level is modifying behavior at the source.

SEED

The source where a change in behavior occurred from positive to negative.

SELF

The idea or construct by which each individual identifies him/herself. It is the method by which individuals determine who they are.

SELF ESTEEM

Feelings of worth based on the value(s) that individuals place on themselves. This is in direct relation to the construct of the self.

SELF SABOTAGE

Deliberate subversion of a particular task or idea in order to prevent dealing with painful thoughts and/or memories or change.

SUBCONSCIOUS MIND

Deepest level of consciousness that affects behavior and houses all good energies that guide and assist in the creation process. Also where the black box is situated.

TRIGGER

A stimulus that creates a powerful response: physical, or emotional – either positive or negative.

Positive- A conditioned response to an uplifting sound, smell, touch or memory that causes a pleasant reaction or experience.

Negative - Response to a sound, smell, touch or memory that causes an unpleasant reaction or experience. Or an automatic emotional response to a perceived verbal or physical attack that causes an individual to experience fear and/or aggressiveness.

UNIVERSE

Energy of creation that manifested the earth. To some this is defined as God.

UP

An emotional state where feelings of positivity and excitement are most prominent.

VACUUM

A space that is created by completing a particular task through which visualizations can manifest using intent.

VISUALIZE

To see, with focus and clarity in the mind's eye, the picture or goal of what one desires to see realized/manifested.

Muneeza Khimji was born and raised in Nairobi, Kenya. She moved to Canada as a teenager for further education where she attended the University of Western Ontario. She then completed her Masters at Brunel University in the United Kingdom. Through her continued education she became a professional life and corporate coach as well as a licensed clinic facilitator. Muneeza is a successful entrepreneur who currently lives between Nairobi and Toronto with her husband.